THE GIFT OF
HEALING

YVETTE JANE

summersdale

THE GIFT OF HEALING

Yvette Jane has asserted her right to be identified as the author of this work in accordance with sections 77 and 78 of the Copyright, Designs and Patents Act 1988.

Summersdale Publishers Ltd
46 West Street
Chichester
West Sussex
PO19 1RP
UK

www.summersdale.com

Printed and bound in the Czech Republic

ISBN: 978-1-84953-607-3

Substantial discounts on bulk quantities of Summersdale books are available to corporations, professional associations and other organisations. For details contact Nicky Douglas by telephone: +44 (0) 1243 756902, fax: +44 (0) 1243 786300 or email: nicky@summersdale.com.

TO...

FROM...

Healing is the process of returning to good health, be it physical, mental or spiritual.

Although the importance of a trained professional cannot be overstated, nobody can know your state of health as well as you can. From encouraging positive thinking in yourself to moving towards a healthier lifestyle, there are many things you can do to help the healing process.

This book is a signpost, pointing the way towards the gift of healing.

If you are feeling blue, make time to watch some of your favourite old comedies. Laughter is an excellent and pain-free remedy.

Endorphins are our bodies' natural happiness chemicals that flow round our blood-stream. By doing more of the activities and pastimes that we enjoy, endorphins help lower our stress levels and give us experiences of pure joy and well-being.

Begin each new day by sitting still for five minutes, connecting with your inner sense of calm and balance. Focus on your breath and allow peace to cascade down your spine and flow throughout your body. An investment of this kind reaps huge benefits for your health and capacity to deal with life's challenges. Onwards you go into your day.

Let go of old resentments. If past choices and regrets lie heavy like stones, you can do nothing except release them and lighten your load. Go for a walk in the garden and while you stride across the earth, visualise every heavy stone falling from your limbs. Notice if your legs feel lighter and jump with joy for the present with its store of new possibilities.

YOU CANNOT TEACH
A MAN ANYTHING,
YOU CAN ONLY HELP
HIM TO FIND IT
WITHIN HIMSELF.

Galileo

Meditation is an excellent way to maintain health and wellness. There are many opportunities to learn through local classes, distant learning courses, books and CDs. Once you have learnt the basics, it is a valuable means of keeping mind, body and soul in balance. Just like a muscle, however, meditation has to be used regularly!

Violets were traditionally utilised for a number of medicinal purposes. Used in teas, oils and ointments they alleviated symptoms in respiratory problems such as bronchitis and coughs, and eased the pain of arthritic joints. These days they are used in the perfume industry and the flowers can be sprinkled on salads and eaten raw. Look out for them flowering in the spring.

Run yourself a bath and add this mixture of aromatherapy oils to nourish and pamper dry skin:

Use four drops of camomile oil, four drops of geranium oil and two drops of patchouli oil. (This blend is suitable for adults; lower quantities can be used to reduce the strength.)

Take notice of your posture – lift your torso upright, check your spine is straight and your shoulder blades are relaxed and lowered. This will automatically improve the flow of air when inhaling and exhaling – give it a go now!

THE GREATEST HEALING THERAPY IS FRIENDSHIP AND LOVE.

Hubert H. Humphrey

Sometimes life depletes us of our energy. How do you recharge your batteries? The best thing to do is develop a connection with your body so that you are aware of your energy levels before they drop to zero. Know which activities help you replenish your energy levels back to full fizz and book some in to your diary.

Try a herbal tea infusion so that your tea break becomes an opportunity to relax and balance your health. Try a mixture of camomile, fennel and marshmallow for a relaxing drink or aniseed, cardamom and liquorice to cleanse and revive.

Imagine yourself surrounded by clear bright light that deflects negativity and allows you to feel positive and loving.

Noise pollution can be difficult to avoid. Whenever you can, choose calm and nurturing music and keep television and radio volumes low. Perhaps put a water feature in your garden to provide a pleasant background sound and encourage more songbirds to visit.

LACK OF ACTIVITY
DESTROYS THE GOOD
CONDITION OF EVERY
HUMAN BEING, WHILE
MOVEMENT AND
METHODICAL PHYSICAL
EXERCISE SAVE IT AND
PRESERVE IT.

Plato

Gregorian chant is religious music of the Middle Ages. It has been found that listening to it results in a quiet mind, steadied pulse and lifted spirits. As with Buddhist mantras, you do not need to have a religious belief; simply enjoy the healing sounds. Download some Gregorian chant and see for yourself.

Stay grounded and be here
in this present moment.

Our response to pain and suffering is often to bury it deeper and pretend it isn't there. Everyone has a wounded child within them so imagine you are cradling this child. Instead of distancing yourself from difficult feelings, look within and be mindful and loving in this moment.

Get bouncing on a rebounder, or mini trampoline. Ten to fifteen minutes daily gives a boost to the lymphatic system, which plays a huge role in maintaining a healthy immune system. This will enable you to stay well while having fun.

THE GREATEST
WEALTH IS HEALTH.

François Fénelon

When faced with difficult challenges, sit and allow yourself to tap in to your inner strength and courage. Know that you have experienced similar things before and remind yourself that you are capable, strong and able to deal with the challenge.

Make your home a healing and tranquil space by clearing clutter and choosing calm colours for the walls. A few carefully chosen items can be a source of inspiration, such as beautiful crystals, plants and flowers.

You are not your thoughts –
be aware that your mind may
tell you negative things, but
you don't have to believe
them. Know that they will
move on, leaving you steady
and balanced.

Think of someone who has caused you some upset. Harbouring ill will towards them doesn't make you feel good. Imagine them standing before you and surround them in healing light. Allow forgiveness to suffuse your heart so that you can feel peaceful again.

THE WORDS OF
KINDNESS ARE
MORE HEALING TO
A DROOPING HEART
THAN BALM OR HONEY.

Sarah Fielding

Keep well watered! Our bodies deteriorate rapidly without water and dehydration is a common cause of tiredness, poor concentration and reduced alertness. Water is an efficient way to flush out toxic matter from your system. The recommendation is eight 200 ml glasses a day.

A sudden crisis can cause you to feel overwhelmed. Bring instant attention to your breath. Notice that it may be tense and shallow, and on the next inhalation slow it right down to the count of seven. Release the exhalation to the count of eleven. Focus on counting a few breaths in this way to improve blood circulation and calm the mind.

If you live in a town, you can remove allergens such as dust, pollen, mould spores, smoke and other pollutants from the air by installing an ioniser in your home or office. This could be either an electric ioniser or a rock salt crystal. It replenishes and recharges the air with negative ions which normally occur naturally by waterfalls, high on mountains or following a lightning storm.

Keep in touch with friends and family. Not only does it keep you happy, but helps to increase your immunity to infection, lowers heart disease risk and reduces mental decline as you age.

HEALING IS A
MATTER OF TIME,
BUT IT IS SOMETIMES
ALSO A MATTER OF
OPPORTUNITY.

Hippocrates

Let good news travel fast! It's beneficial for your well-being to share your happiness. It fosters close relationships and it feels good to get positive responses from others.

Give yourself the gift of silence for 15 minutes. Go somewhere you can be completely quiet and top up your composure.

It's time to deal with past sorrows. Imagine they are weighing you down in heavy old suitcases. Let them go. You don't need that baggage any more!

Gardening can be very therapeutic and uplifting. Plant plenty of bulbs in advance to appear in late winter and early spring. Include snowdrops, daffodils, narcissi, crocuses and tulips. They are a welcome sight after the dark and cold, heralding the warmth and light of longer days.

A MAN TOO BUSY
TO TAKE CARE OF
HIS HEALTH IS LIKE
A MECHANIC TOO
BUSY TO TAKE CARE
OF HIS TOOLS.

Spanish proverb

It's easy to spend too much time pleasing other people through their demands and expectations. Set your boundaries and your goals and start pleasing yourself instead.

Choose to do the things that energise you and spark your passion. Listening to your inner preferences is important for living the life you truly wish to have.

Nobody is perfect. Accept your own imperfections and know that you are not inferior to anyone else. Lovingly encourage yourself and believe that you are good enough.

Set your own pace –
in a composed and
serene manner.

ALTHOUGH THE
WORLD IS FULL OF
SUFFERING, IT IS
FULL ALSO OF THE
OVERCOMING OF IT.

Helen Keller

Don't just tap your feet to the music, get up and dance. Your body loves to move so let it groove!

Lavender oil has numerous healing properties. It is known to help relieve headaches, insomnia, tension and sunburned skin. It can be used to clean cuts and skin irritations. It has a regulating and harmonising effect on the nervous system and can have a tonic or sedative effect, depending on how you are feeling. Buy yourself a little bottle and enjoy its versatility as well as its calming aroma.

Reciting words or mantras can have a healing effect. Well-known phrases from the Tibetan Buddhists include *'Om mani padme hum'*. These words mean compassion for all beings, human and animal. Make up your own phrases to bring to mind whenever you feel the need, such as 'I am calm and all is well.' Repeat them slowly to yourself and feel rested and centred.

Remember to ask for help
when you need it.

THE ONLY WAY OUT OF THE LABYRINTH OF SUFFERING IS TO FORGIVE.

John Green

Even when you are in a busy city you can still connect to nature. Remember that beneath the concrete there is the rich earth and nearby there are trees, parks and ponds. Beyond the city is the countryside and the places you may love to replenish your thoughts with. Visualise green landscapes, mountains or the sea and remember this whenever you are feeling frazzled with urban living.

As you wash your hands during the day, give your full attention to massaging the handwash and warm water across your skin. Enjoy the pleasant sensations and the aroma, being grateful for all the things your hands enable you to do.

When you feel distressed or negative, imagine yourself cradling your heart with kindness and love. This compassionate approach will allow you to move through the discomfort and foster healing more quickly.

Your body has the ability to get you back into balance after a stressful experience. Learning to manage your stress is an essential life skill and bringing awareness to your breath is the most accessible tool in your control.

YOUR OWN SELF-
REALISATION IS THE
GREATEST SERVICE
YOU CAN RENDER
THE WORLD.

Ramana Maharshi

Take a break from that task
that is causing you stress.
Move away to something
else for 15 minutes and
return refreshed with a
clearer head.

Surround yourself with cheerful colours, pleasing textures, fresh scents and beautiful objects. We are affected both positively and negatively by everything, so take charge of what you can.

Make small positive changes towards better health. This could mean introducing a short walk every day and reducing the number of snacks you have. Start noticing the benefits of feeling happier and rejuvenated within a short space of time.

Where the mind goes the body follows. Sit comfortably with closed eyes and imagine you are sweeping a wave of relaxation throughout your body.

EVERYBODY NEEDS
BEAUTY AS WELL AS
BREAD, PLACES TO
PLAY IN AND PRAY
IN, WHERE NATURE
MAY HEAL AND GIVE
STRENGTH TO BODY
AND SOUL ALIKE.

John Muir

Gently cradle your wrist inside your free hand. Use your thumb to massage your inner wrist. This is a soothing way to relieve stress and tension for anyone who routinely uses their wrists in repetitive movements, such as typing at the computer.

Melt tension by allowing yourself to think of pleasurable moments. You may be standing on a crowded train but by focusing on an enjoyable thought, you can guide the warm and glowing feelings through the whole of your body. Your journey can be transformed and you will arrive at your destination completely relaxed.

Use positive thinking patterns to change the beliefs you have about you and your life. Take charge of creating the life you want.

You can slow down the pace of your day by opening up moments of quiet calm. There is the opportunity to spend a minute of calm stillness while the kettle boils, your computer is switching on or before setting off in your car.

ACCEPT WHAT IS, LET GO OF WHAT WAS, AND HAVE FAITH IN WHAT WILL BE.

Sonia Ricotti

On a clear bright night, allow your gaze to rest on the star-filled night sky. It relaxes your body and mind and helps to put all your worries into perspective.

We all need periods of retreat to regenerate and nourish ourselves before moving on again. These can take the form of cosy withdrawal to our homes on winter evenings or a slow-paced summer holiday. Make plans for your year to incorporate these invaluable times of replenishment.

Walk barefoot on grass or sand. Imagine letting negative feelings and ill-health flow through your toes to the earth below and invite the replenishing energy of nature to reinvigorate you.

Something as simple as a hot-water bottle can be very therapeutic. Next time you are feeling tired and under the weather snuggle up with yours!

HOPE IS BEING ABLE
TO SEE THAT THERE IS
LIGHT DESPITE ALL OF
THE DARKNESS.

Desmond Tutu

Keep anxiety at bay with a crystal palm stone in your pocket. It is designed to fit into the palm of your hand and stroking its polished texture can be reassuring in moments of stress.

Tibetan or Himalayan singing bowls are used widely in prayer, meditation and healing. When they are struck with a special stick the resounding vibrations relieve tension and promote a great sense of well-being. The bowls themselves can be made from a variety of materials such as copper, bronze and quartz crystal. Look out for sound healing sessions to go along to and experience.

Warm glowing feelings really do happen when you think about, observe or practise an act of kindness because this stimulates the vagus nerve, connected to the heart. Dopamine is also released from the brain, associated with sensations that feel like a natural high. So be kind – it's good for you!

Allow yourself a certain amount of time each day to worry about the things you feel you must. Once your worry time is over, set your anxiety aside until the next scheduled time. It can make things feel manageable and frees you up to focus on happier thoughts.

EAT WELL, DRINK IN
MODERATION AND
SLEEP SOUND. IN
THESE THREE GOOD
HEALTH ABOUND.

Latin proverb

A quick fix of refined sugar releases insulin into your body eliciting a temporary rush of happiness which ends all too quickly. Better food choices to improve mood are spinach, cauliflower and tuna, rich in vitamin B6, and bananas, almonds and broccoli, packed with magnesium.

Be responsible for listening to your own self. Identify your intuitive thoughts, your body's messages and your emotional needs. Value the wealth of information you find and respect your unique inner guidance.

Falling water creates naturally healthier air by splitting air particles to become mainly negatively charged. This is why it is refreshing to walk by the ocean or a waterfall. A simple way to breathe replenished ionised air is when you shower. It can provide part of your routine in maintaining good health.

If you are feeling stressed, burn a candle or tea light in a blue-coloured glass holder. The candlelight is soft and gentle and the blue glow has a calming effect. Sit in stillness and relax, letting your eyes rest on the flickering flame.

So many people spend their health gaining wealth, and then have to spend their wealth to regain their health.

A. J. Materi

Try to be active every day when it comes to exercise. If you drive somewhere regularly, park a little further away or get off the bus a stop early so that you experience a short walk as part of your routine.

At sunset, stand outside facing west. Allow yourself to feel your worries and despondency and as the sun begins to sink, visualise all those negative thoughts sinking away with it. Remember that all things are temporary and tomorrow is a new day.

Adequate sleep is essential for replenishing mind, body and spirit. Limit television and computer use as early in the evening as you can to generate the body's own reposeful response. Create a soothing bedtime routine with warm drinks, relaxing baths and calming music.

Use a dry body brush with natural bristles to boost your lymphatic system. This in turn keeps your immune system working healthily.

'HEALING,' PAPA
WOULD TELL ME, 'IS
NOT A SCIENCE, BUT
THE INTUITIVE ART OF
WOOING NATURE.'

W. H. Auden

Be still. Be silent. Be present.
Allow your body to be
in repose. Give yourself
healing moments of
replenishment through
the act of simply being.

Garlic-rich diets may affect your breath, but have numerous health benefits. The active ingredients in garlic are as beneficial and powerful as antibiotics, reduce high cholesterol levels and balance blood pressure. If you want to gain the benefits without the odour, try garlic capsules.

Identify your body's reactions to stress so you can find the best activities to alleviate them. If you get angry or agitated under stress, look for ways to experience calm through meditation or a yoga class. If you withdraw or become depressed under stress, find activities that energise you, such as running or a dance session.

If you are recovering from illness make sure you have clothing that feels soft against your skin or a special blanket to wrap round you for comfort. The tiniest of things can help lift the spirits and nurture you back to full health.

GROWTH BEGINS
WHEN WE BEGIN
TO ACCEPT OUR
WEAKNESSES.

Jean Vanier

Expressing gratitude can have profound effects on your health and mood. Keep a daily note of things that you are grateful for and after ten weeks of this, you can expect to have fewer health complaints and feel increased goodwill towards others.

There is something very healing about singing every day. Ten minutes of singing helps relieve symptoms of stress, clears sinuses and improves your posture. Singing with others can be an enlivening experience – join a local group who sing for fun and enrich your life with new friends as well as good health.

Warm some drops of bergamot essential oil on a burner to release the uplifting aroma derived from the small orange-like fruits. Not only is the fragrance restorative, it has strong antiseptic properties too.

Reignite your sense of wonder by visiting a bird reserve. Grab a pair of binoculars and spend a few hours watching a variety of birds. Their plumage, sounds and busy activity can be fascinating to experience close at hand. Leave with a sense of contentment and connection to nature.

THE TIME TO RELAX IS WHEN YOU DON'T HAVE TIME FOR IT.

Sydney J. Harris

A mixture of a few drops of camomile and lavender aromatherapy oils can be added to sweet almond oil and used on the skin. Ask a friend to massage your neck and shoulder area with this soothing mixture, bringing relief to tense muscles and tired joints.

We tend to store negative emotions within us and these pop up when we find ourselves in challenging situations. Next time you react in anger or carelessness, be aware of your reactions. This is the first step on a journey of healing.

Become aware of your feet and their connection to the ground. When we do this we allow the earth to absorb our unwanted feelings such as fears and anxieties. We also remember that we are held up and supported by this strong foundation that we may call Mother Earth.

Smile! It sets in motion a positive response in your body and before you know it, you feel happy!

THE GREATEST GLORY
IN LIVING LIES NOT IN
NEVER FALLING, BUT
IN RISING EVERY
TIME WE FALL.

Nelson Mandela

Remember an occasion when you felt joyful. Allow those feelings of happiness, like a warm glowing sun, to be breathed all around your body. Sense every cell filling with contented joyous bliss.

Spending time relaxing is essential to energise your immune system and ward off illness. Find some quick and easy ways to relax, which you can implement every day. These may include progressive relaxation exercises, yoga poses, listening to calming music or walking in nature.

A mindful check-in can be done any time when you first arrive somewhere new. Simply bring your focus to your body, noting where you may be holding any aches and tensions. Notice what emotions are present. Acknowledge how you are, then move onwards with greater clarity and awareness having completed this minute of self-care.

Be kind to yourself – we are frequently kinder to others than we are to ourselves! Give some thought to what kindness to yourself might mean, then give it a go.

THE BODY IS LIKE A
PIANO, AND HAPPINESS
IS LIKE MUSIC. IT IS
NEEDFUL TO HAVE THE
INSTRUMENT IN
GOOD ORDER.

Henry Ward Beecher

If you want to give up a habit that is not good for your health, start by becoming aware of your cravings. Notice how your body feels as the need for something arises and you seem to feel powerless in its hold. Know that this feeling will subside. All things pass and in another moment you may feel differently.

You can reduce food binges and overeating by consuming your meals without distractions. Create calm surroundings in which to fully savour your meal. You will become more aware of how much food you are eating and the flavours will be greatly enhanced.

If you suffer from daily aches and pains, sit mindfully with them. Observe the sensations and become aware of the qualities you identify. This has the effect of lessening the power that the pain has over you. Find a local class or distance learning course to learn about mindfulness and how it can be used to help manage chronic pain.

Hooray for apples! Their benefits are numerous. Eaten regularly they are excellent detoxifiers, they lower cholesterol levels, maintain strong teeth and gums and alleviate indigestion and other digestive disorders.

THE BEST PLACE TO FIND A HELPING HAND IS AT THE END OF YOUR OWN ARM.

Swedish proverb

Owning a pet can lower your blood pressure and heart rate and help with depression. Care for your pet with plenty of exercise, grooming and playing. This enhances your mood, keeps you fit and most of all, it's enjoyable. Your pet will love you too!

Spend a quiet half hour with the lights down and candles gently glowing while you lie down and focus on your breathing. Give yourself the gift of rest and repose.

Sit facing your partner with your knees touching. Centre yourselves with a few deep breaths and begin to look directly into each other's eyes. Hold their gaze and spend a few minutes in this way giving undivided attention. It's OK to smile or cry – simply allow emotions to arise and at the end you can hug one another and chat about this healing experience if you wish.

If you are recovering from illness, visualise a cocoon of the colour blue surrounding you with its energetic properties of healing and wholeness. Imagine you are breathing it in, and with each breath its warming glow flows through every cell of your body and reverberates with wellness.

A KIND GESTURE CAN
REACH A WOUND THAT
ONLY COMPASSION
CAN HEAL.

Steve Maraboli

Feeling guilty doesn't change a situation. Forgive yourself for any wrongdoing and learn from your experience. Move on with a lighter heart.

Music therapy is used in hospitals to manage pain and boost general well-being. Notice which kinds of music lift your spirits. Allow the melodies to fill your senses and banish the blues.

Have you ever tried a floatation tank? The salty water replicates the Dead Sea and allows you to float as if on air. It is said to be the most relaxing thing possible. Alternatively, try a hot tub which has an element of buoyancy. Its strategically placed jets are aimed at the muscle groups to increase blood flow and reduce muscle strain and tension throughout your body. Enjoy and relax!

Experiences like loss and pain are cyclical. Just as the harsh winter moves on to become springtime, so do our experiences shift and revolve with time. Allow yourself to flow with this cycle of life.

GO INTO YOURSELF
AND SEE HOW DEEP
THE PLACE IS FROM
WHICH YOUR LIFE
FLOWS.

Rainer Maria Rilke

Sit and watch the sea. The tranquil blue or the pounding stormy waves are like human emotions. They are changeable and ever-flowing. Allow the storms of your life to pass through and know that calm will always follow.

Focus on your breathing. Say to yourself as you breathe, 'I breathe in peace. I breathe out calm.'

Open your heart to life. Do this by visualising your heart as a rosebud and when you wish to be open-hearted, imagine the rose blooming open with its beautiful petals. When you feel you need to withdraw, turn your rose back into a bud.

Accept yourself. You are
doing the best you can.

SLEEP IS THAT
GOLDEN CHAIN THAT
TIES HEALTH AND OUR
BODIES TOGETHER.

Thomas Dekker

Each breath taken
replenishes and restores
every cell in the body.

Much of our suffering stems from our minds regurgitating the past or worrying about the future. As this takes place in our minds, it is the very same place for healing. By becoming conscious of our negative self-talk we have the choice to tell ourselves something different; that we are strong, calm, capable and marvellous in this present moment.

Everything is impermanent.
This can be a comforting
reminder if you are
suffering with depression
or grief. Know that healing
comes with patience and
the passing of time.

Surround yourself with friends and people who are positive, fun and loving. Life can be tough and their support will sometimes be a necessary gift.

EVENTUALLY, YOU
WILL COME TO
UNDERSTAND
THAT LOVE HEALS
EVERYTHING, AND
LOVE IS ALL THERE IS.

Gary Zukav

Reflexology is an effective way to relieve tension and stress, balance the body and improve nerve and blood supply by working on the feet, and sometimes the hands. It is said to help alleviate a range of conditions and injuries, allergies and illnesses and works in a gentle yet powerful way. Put your best foot forward and find out if it's for you!

Think gentle thoughts – we can be hard on ourselves sometimes with our inner talk telling us we 'should', 'have to' and 'must'. Replace these orders with a kindlier attitude, saying to yourself, 'I choose to do this', 'I may do that' or 'I have time to do that.'

ALL HEALING IS FIRST A HEALING OF THE HEART.

Carl Townsend